SANDGRAIN AND HOURGLASS

PENELOPE SHUTTLE

SANDGRAIN
AND
HOURGLASS

BLOODAXE BOOKS

ISBN: 978 1 85224 882 6

First published 2010 by
Bloodaxe Books Ltd,
Highgreen,
Tarset,
Northumberland NE48 1RP.

www.bloodaxebooks.com
For further information about Bloodaxe titles
please visit our website or write to
the above address for a catalogue.

Supported by
**ARTS COUNCIL
ENGLAND**

Cover design: Neil Astley & Pamela Robertson-Pearce.

Printed in Great Britain by
Bell & Bain Limited, Glasgow, Scotland.

For my mother Joan, for my daughter Zoe

&

*remembering Peter Redgrove, Jack Shuttle,
and Linda Smith*

ACKNOWLEDGEMENTS

Thanks are due to the following magazines, anthologies and websites which first published some of these poems: *Answering Back, Branchlines, Eye Wear, Lapidus Newsletter, Pratik, poetrybay.com, Poetry Ireland Review, Poetry London, Poetry Review, Poetry Wales, The Manhattan Review, The Rialto, The Wolf, Artemis, Spring, Stony Thursday, Warwick Review, www.poetryinternational.org.*

'To a Singing Master' was recorded for the Oxfam CD *Lifelines 2*. 'Taking Out the Drip' was published in *Il Fiacre* in an Italian translation by Caterina De Nardi. An extract from 'The Keening' was broadcast in *The Male Muse* on BBC Radio 4. 'Old Explorer' was commissioned by Tate Etc and appeared on their website as Poem of the Month in September 2009.

My grateful thanks to the Authors' Foundation for a grant in 2009, and to the Hawthornden Foundation for a fellowship in 2005 where early drafts of some of these poems were written.

Special thanks go to Michael Bayley for his valued comments, and likewise to the members of The Falmouth Poetry Group and The Poetry Project.

CONTENTS

Each Tear

Each tear recognised me,
knew me from long ago

It was as if I'd never been away

Now they could flow again,
they could keep an eye on my sorrow

To a Singing Master

But who shaved, washed
and dressed you for the pyre?

Did they handle you gently,
or treat you like a piece of meat?

(Were we not one flesh?)

Who cut and sewed your shroud?
Was it clean?   Was it threadbare?

Who slammed back the doors,
raked out the ashes?

Ah my singing master,
who sings to you now?

The Keening

Yo voy a cerrar los ojos

I close my eyes –
I can see you better like this,
your head and high-domed brow,

your sea-green eye,
your eyelid, patient eyelash.

You are lost to me forever
but I am looking
at your *canst no more* temple,

your ear crammed full of silence,
singer's blank mouth,
lips, the upper, the lower,
their rue and rowan.

I feast my closed eyes
on your jaw, throat and neck,
your shoulder turned forever from the wheel,
your right arm so quietly past its prime.

Ah slowcoach,
how clearly I see
your clean-pared fingernails,
your strong wrist,

and resting heart – the vial of your heart
so long our wellkept secret...

I can't bear to look there,
even through closed eyes,
nor contemplate the rapids of your bloodstream
stemmed forever,

so I gaze at all your dear limbs...

Mine is the hard scrutiny
of the aubergiste looking down
at the small-change tip in her hand,
(though I keep no inn),
or of the captain searching no man's land
for snipers, were I a warrior.

I look at your flanks
where my smoothing hand so often lingered,
loving your human body,
and at your sex
to which we gave no nickname,
at your skin's familiar landmarks,
frecks and specks and brindles –

I yearn over the vineyard of you...
not forgetting to look
at thigh, poor knee and calf,
your feet Time is not fit to wash.

Your bones, the fallen mast of your spine,
yes, those also I see –

I'm forbidden to touch you,
for we're no longer one flesh;

I may not give you a kiss of life,
nor my westerly bring joy of rain

to your parchlands,
but I am allowed this second sight of grief.

Day and night I look –
your head, your heel, your heart –
for love blindfolded is love still.

This looking is what is called mourning,
and this is how I have learned to mourn.

The Scattering

I cast you into the waters.
Be lake, or random moon.

Be first light,
lifting up its beggar's cup.

I scatter your ashes.
Be the gale teaching autumn
to mend its ways,
or leopard so proud of his spotted coat.

Be the mentor of cherry trees.

I cast your dust far and wide,
a sower broadcasting seed:
Be wild rose or hellebore or all-heal.

Descend as a vein of silver,
never to be seen,
deep in the lynx-eyed earth.

Rise as barn owl white as dusk;
dove or raven marvelling at his flight.
Know different delights.

The Repose of Baghdad

If we ever meet again,
and I don't see how we can,
it won't be on the Avenida del Poeta Rilke
in Ronda,
or by the banks of the green Guadalquivir
or in Granada
where the sunset goes on till midnight,
it won't be in any of those houses by the sea
we called our own,
or in the Plaza Abul Beka
where the house martins feed their fledglings
in mud-nests under the sills,
or in the square
where the foal above the fountain
watches his moon shadow
on the wall of an inn old when Cervantes knew it,
and it won't be up in the mountains
where at the hottest hour of the day
one hundred thin long-faced wild sheep
pour out of a cave, as from the underworld.

If I ever see you again
it won't be in the water mirrors
of the Alhambra
or in a building
that doesn't know if it's a cathedral
or a mosque
or by the fountains of the Garden of the Poets
in the Alcazar Real
or in the dark oratory
where they keep the writing bones
of St Juan de la Cruz, gift-wrapped
in white ribbons.

And if I ever travel north,
you won't be sitting beside me
on the bus to Silverknowles,
Clovenhorn or Rosewell.

If I ever sleep with you again
it won't be in our own eager bed
or in that haunted hotel four-poster at Glastonbury,
on the drunken sleeper to Paddington
or on board the QE2 well below the waterline,

we won't sleep together
in any friend's spare bed
or on a neighbour's floor
after some burst pipe emergency
or in that hilarious sleepless bed
of our first year together,

no, if we ever meet again
(and how can we?)
it will be in a summer time has lost track of,
in a back-street *hostal*
hidden in a labyrinth of tiny white lanes,

two steps past the old Synagogue
and the dens of the silversmiths,
within the white walls
and behind the black window grilles
of *The Repose of Baghdad*,
still bearing – see it? –
its faded sign of star and crescent moon.

Taking the Drip Out

Then one afternoon
in a little private office
the consultant tells Zoe and me
there's no more to be done for you,

they're going to remove
the feeding drip, up the drug dosage,
'and he'll just slip away'.

Already high on a flying carpet
of kindly morphine dreams,
you've nothing more to say to us,
though last week you could still moan,

'get me out of here'.

In the corridor the junior doctor
asks furtively,
'if he has a coronary arrest,
do you want him resuscitated?'

Unanswerable question –
a few feet away, on your deathbed,
you're letting go the autumns of the future,

remembering maybe
how years ago I charmed your wart away,
pressing a lump of raw steak to your cheek,
reciting,
'O wen, wen, o little wennikins,
Here shall you build not, here have no abode...'
before burying the chunk of meat
in the north of our garden...

Maybe you dreamed of our modest travels.
Like Rembrandt, you never visited Rome.
Like the Master of the Small Landscape
you loved the microcosmic –
                sandgrains, water droplets,
                chips of granite, the exact quota of crystals
                packed into a geode no bigger than an egg.

On the day they take the drip out
there's so much we don't know,
how it will be your first-born,
not me or your last-born

who'll be holding your hand
as you slip away;
we don't know how hard
the world door will slam shut after you go;

above all we don't know,
Zoe and I,
how beautiful and welcoming
the sunlit sands of Maenporth will be

(o come unto these yellow sands)

nor how the equinoctial blue sky
will watch over us,
like a witty person struck silent,
as I scatter your ashes into the bright waves,
and the sea, nature's perfectionist,
bears you away in triumph.

Edward San

Some quiet person
is translating the poems of Edward Thomas
into Japanese.

Now it rains in orchards
in the land of the haiku.

The bird of the snow
is flying over Tokyo.

A pure thrush word
spreads its calligraphic wings
over Kyoto,

an unknown bird
whistles his three lovely notes
in the woods near Kiwa-Cho.

All Japan's cherry trees
shed their petals
on the old road to Hiroshima,

where no one comes for a wedding.
The bullet train
doesn't stop at Japan's Adlestrop,

but all the birds of Japan's
North Island and South Island
go on singing.

Someone is alone
in the new house at Osaka
when the wind begins to moan,

a child with his mother
on the cliffs at Morioka
hears the bell ringing under the sea

and in the mountain gardens
of Kobe, Sapporo and Hokkaido
readers are spellbound

by two voices,
the wind and the rain.

London, Pregnant

By the end of summer,
    these last August days,
        so hot, cloudy and canine,

London is massive,
    very advanced in pregnancy,
        one enormous *ouff*-belly,

every nubile woman
    big and wise as an elephant,
        vastly expectant,

lumbering onto buses
    and trains,
        all clad in maternity lycra

stretched so tightly
    over each gigantic belly
        the navel

stands out
    like a baby thumb
        stuck out hitching through the belly wall,

hey, you can practically
    see the rest of the child
        deeply engaged within –

So big with child a city,
    so close to term
        I'm surprised

the streets aren't full
    of women squatting in labour
        or cradling

their bloodied unsullied young
    at the breast
        or biting through the sinewy

nutritious cord
    before flinging it
        to the pavement pigeons –

all London
    one mass wail of newborns
        drowning out the sirens

of police cars
    blundering at top speed
        through uncaring traffic –

every child
    named in gratitude
        for the passing tourist

pressed
    into unexpected
        spontaneous midwifery –

Jorge, Wolfgang,
    Marinka, Li Yang,
        or after the café or shop

in which birth occurred,
    Costa, Strada,
        Claire, East.

Machine

I invent a machine for grading kisses
on an approximate scale of $1-20$

rising from (1) the air kiss on the social cheek,
to the routine kiss (4) exchanged by a pair

of experienced adulterers,
the unskilled but energetic kisses (9) of adolescents,

the nose kiss (12) given to a weary old cat,
the French kiss (14)

people are giving other people all over the world
to (20) the fieriest Don Juan kiss in all Seville

But kisses the old Soviets gave
on the Mayday parade dais in Moscow,

kisses leaving a trail of destruction
in their wake,
are unacceptable,

this machine does not have a Judas function,
take those anti-kisses away.

To the eager petit machine,
(didn't I say? you carry it in your pocket
like a Blackberry)

I bring two kisses, our first, our last —
the machine's dial tells me

they are of equal value,
grades them beyond grading;

there will always be off-the-scale kisses like this,
I realise,
if we are lucky, if we are bereft.

The Childhood of Snow

This strange child visits restless lakes,
thoughtful mountains,

this child is always elsewhere –
sends me few messages

I know them all by heart

This child locks the gates of Warsaw,
has a pet deer for her beast of burden,
masterminds
the blossoming of the whitest hawthorn ever,

flies round the earth five times,
like a swift, vanishing
into her own delight.

You

Now there's no trace of you anywhere,
and you're no longer interested in me
or that equally private creature, the moon,

I'm like someone so far behind with the rent
not even her great grandchildren
will be able to settle the debt –

But sometimes your absence hovers
close to me in the form of a hummingbird

whose bright wings beat the rain into so many rainbows
I'm like the river drinking from her own cupped hands...

Bedtime

Sometimes, in a domestic crisis,
you'd shrug, adopt a joke accent –

I'm joost a leetel happy, joost a leetel sad...

hoping to jog me out of my crankiness,
offering me (as I well knew), a tender heart.

Sometimes I shrugged back, laughed,
but too often rejected your offering.

If by some magic, you could be here again,
I'd stick my hand out
through the bars of my cage of scalding tears
to accept your gift.

If you could be here at midnight to say –
Isn't it time we were in bed?
I wouldn't be up half the night,
beloved, wayward with loneliness.

Sandgrain and Hourglass

Your summer wishes me well.
My sunset rushes off without a word.

You rule over a Byzantium of nettles.
I tell them rain's unfinished story.

You're dust and ashes.
My Honours List bears only your name.

I climb your castle in the air.
You listen to my stay-at-home fairytale.

You have your sandgrain
and your sorrow.

I have my hourglass
and my grief.

Look at us –
so far apart, so conjoined

no one may shed
a single tear between us.

Grief

1 *Keeper*

He's the keeper of my wardrobe,
repairs my coat of shining mail,
warms my iron slippers,
wraps me all winter in a leaden cloak

Wherever I travel,
he packs my bronze gowns,
blue-steel shellsuit and copper cardigan,
garments forged not sewn

Only Grief is strong enough
to lug my suitcase out to the car –
Surely, he says,
you will not go naked?

2 *On his shoulders*

As always Grief turns away,
because I have too-sorrow a heart

Nowadays
I have neither sun nor moon,
and weep for hours, like Pyotr Illych,

because Grief no longer carries me
on his broad shoulders,

but takes ship for Mecca,

not caring if I suffer for days,
like a woman in old-fashioned childbed,

or a far-north river
taking ten months of the year to wake up,

like autumn
hoping against hope to be spring,

or *Summer making her light escape*

Looking Back

Rain knuckled down over The Lizard
clean as any small language

the day we saw a bunch of house keys
tied to the silver-leaf tree.

Was that the proud first day of October 1976,
my lover,
or the well-born seventh of Genver 2000?

The loneliest day of February,
or May's wise little Sunday?

Our extended family of sighs
can't remember,
nor can I from my office in your footprint.

> Remember how the sun leapt across The Lizard
> in a great hoodoo of joy?

> Was that on the tenth of Hope,
> or on the fifth of Kiss?

No matter.

I don't care if today's the Broken Window
of March 30th
or the Nothing of June,

because I know you drink from my sober glass
as song drinks,
thirsty from breaking his long silence.

In that brilliant rainy westward light,
keys shone, leaves glittered,
we had our free and easy day.

(Now all day the day studies me in silence,
does not know what to do next...)

Genver: January.

Gansey

HAPPY SEPTEMBER !
WHAT A GREAT MONTH
TO START KNITTING A SWEATER!

Once only fishermen wore the Gansey,
        extreme-weather garment
                knitted in one piece on five steel needles
from the tightly-spun 5 ply wool
        called *Seaman's Iron*,
                tightly knotted so as to *turn water* –
the lack of seams ensuring greater strength
                and impermeability,
                        the underarm gusset allowing
freedom of movement,
                the lower sleeves left plain
                    · to be unravelled and re-knitted
when worn-out,
                while the patterning across the chest
                    provides extra insulation –
Note that the patterning is the same
        back and front, so that areas of heavier wear,
                such as the elbows,
can be alternated –
        it never goes out of fashion,
                nowadays anyone can wear one,
knitted in mad untraditional colours,
        Crushed Raspberry or Herring Girl Pink,
                flaunting your gansey
                    miles from the coast,
                            Paris, London, or Rome

This close-up
of a Filey pattern
shows the diamonds
(representing nets),
cables and herringbones
and although the knitting
looks complicated
it is simply a mixture
of knit and purl stitches
as well as the cable –
                no, the real art
                of Gansey knitting
                is the skill
                needed to wield five double-ended
                steel needles –
it is possible
to use a circular knitting needle
for the smaller sizes
but the number of stitches
required for larger sizes (300)
                and the weight of the wool
                means that only steel pins
                provide a satisfactory arm-aching result;
                the other requirement is patience –
            each Gansey takes at least a month to complete –

Mon Dieu, le gansey!
    ce tricote avec de la laine 5 ply bleu tres fonce!

Many of the age-old stitch motifs
            used to decorate ganseys
                    are inspired by everyday objects –
ropes, anchors, nets, pebbles on the shore,
            herringbones – the only limit
                    to the design of a gansey

is the knitter's imagination – patterns of weather,
   shapes made by the waves, flashes of lightning,
      church windows, hens' claws, hailstones,
and of course the ubiquitous *zigzag* pattern
   representing
      the ups and downs of married life –

(that broader non-marital zigzag
      is called
            the multitude going up the mountain)

I don't want a Swedish North Halland Pullover,
or a Swedish Ullared
or a Norwegian Setesdal Lusekofte,
or a Danish Sejero Skratroy
or a Hyjaltland Vest – I want a Gansey

And though you say
   you wouldn't be seen dead in one,
      a good many folk were –
         how else do you think
            they identified shipwrecked fishermen
               washed up all along the British coast?

Miss Child's Owl

Miss Child calls her brown wood owl *Ruth*,
because her sister, Mrs Rivers, objects
to her first choice, Eve.

After missing their last train home,
Miss Child, Mrs Rivers and Ruth
stay at a cheap hotel by London Bridge.

They have no luggage,
just the owl.

Miss Child and her married sister
get no sleep at all
because of Ruth's noisy hooting.

Miss Child tucks Ruth up the sooty chimney,
then in front of the mirror,
then finally,

in weary despair,
at the centre of a circle of lit candles,
to trick Ruth

into thinking it is sunlight.
No chance.
Back into her basket goes Ruth.

But she soon bursts out
and wings round the room for angry hours,
whoo whoo whoo.

At first light,
Miss Child wakes up a waiter,
asks for some live mice.

Ah, this is a mistake.

Your Portrait

A hundred times a day
    I pass your portrait in the hall
        without a second glance

Today
    I stop in my tracks,
        twist on the spit of grief

I thought my weeping days were over and done,
    but these tears
        are fresh as paint,

your image dashed on the canvas
    more than I can bear,
        more than your bed, desk, typewriter,

lamp, reading glasses can bear,
    poor puzzled things,
        not knowing where you are, dear master,
            or where you've gone...

Your adversary painted this oil sketch of you
    back in the sixties –
        he was your best friend,

hadn't yet found out
    you were having an affair
        with his boozy multipara chess-champion wife

X was a womaniser
    feared
        the length and breadth of Leeds –

it made no difference,
    he never spoke to you again.
        Thirty years later, a widower,

he sent you his book (no note enclosed) –
    charcoal drawings of every cathedral
        in England and Wales, a rage of dark shadings

But he depicted you in fire colours,
    a furnace palette, your face half-turned to us,
        uneasy in a godsend of red and gold,

your brow's fierce tranquillity
    a swelter of brushwork
        When you sat for him,

he saw the fire of poetry in you,
    missed the fire of a first-time adulterer's glee
        Who but this fellow artist

showed you
    how to slip through the cracks in a marriage,
        lost you wife and children,

brought you, all unknowing, to me?
    You loved that book of wild cathedrals,
        never responded to the thrown-down gauntlet of it...

A hundred times a day
    I pass your portrait in the hall...

Telling the Time

I tell time
by the kingfisher's swoop above the river.

I set my watch
by the woodpecker's countdown to noon.

The first humble-bee's too early.
The wood anemones arrive a day late.

I don't carry a cage of goldfinches on my head,
like a Kabul woman.

I don't have a baby swaddled
in a treetrunk cradle, like a woman from Lapland.

Desire still lifts me on its silvers and silences
despite the memory
of our one bitter quarrel on Gracechild Street.

I tell time by the river's minute.
I set my watch by the cloud-hour at the window.

Hope never makes a guest appearance,
not even to examine the plain washed bowls
stacked and left to dry on the dish-rack,

or to exclaim at the kingfisher's blue haste
or hear the woodpecker nagging me – hurry!

Why hurry? I've got all the time in the world,
haven't I, Peter,
to etch our story on time's clean slate?

Like St Agnes

Like St Agnes
    carrying her severed breasts to heaven
        on a tray,
or a faithless queen
    tucking her beheaded head under her arm
        for all eternity,
I can't get over myself,
    carrying my heart wrapped in newspaper
        across Europe,
torn from me by your last words –
    have a nice time – whispered to me
        as the two kind burly men stowed you in the ambulance –
What malevolent goblin's spell
    kept me from riding with you to Casualty?
        Did I really think you'd be back in a couple of hours,
                kissed all better?
I'm carrying my heart everywhere,
    such a lump, trailing blood
        No wonder they frown me through Customs –
I've learned the hard way,
    what it means to be *heart-less* –
        Grief caught me red-handed,
that's why my heart aches so,
    even though it's rip't from my flesh –
        and why I pity not The Maid of Orléans
but the one who set her pyre aflame,
    the heartless one,
        who will never stop burning.

I Think It Will Happen Like This

Returning from a long hard shop
    at Tesco's,
        I'll be lugging my carriers

in out of the rain,
    wondering where the day's gone,
        when you call from your study –

    Is that you, Agent Mulder?

Or coming down
    from my early-evening quiet time
        in the attic

I'll find the supper cooked,
    you presiding in the kitchen
        over one of your simple practical meals,

every pan, dish and spatula we own
    stacked, unwashed, in a bowl
        of greasy lukewarm water.

Or rounding the corner
    of the rampart at Pendennis Castle
        I'll see you ahead of me,

impatient for your tea and scone
    in the café,
        or find you settled down

in the reserved seat next to mine at Truro,
    having boarded the London train
        five stations earlier at Penzance.

Or perhaps,
    just as the film begins
        you'll tap me on the shoulder, leaning from the row behind.

When I open our front door to four impatient rings
    I want to find you, fuming, your keys
        in your other jacket.

Let me roll up at the dentist –
    ah, there you are, in the waiting room,
        your toothache far worse than mine.

Or in a village in Spain,
    you'll be tending your olive trees,
        marshalling your goats,

and I won't be surprised, nor you.
    Of course.
        Of course.

Old Explorer

Pablo Picasso, Femme nue au collier, *Tate Modern*

You create me
    in one furious day,
        you old soul-snatcher

You fling me on the canvas,
    beating off old age
        in angry brushstrokes,

on the eve
    of your eighty-seventh birthday,
        not asking me

if I want
    this vulgar river
        spouting from my sex,

or even more rude,
    to be depicted nude,
        visible farts chuntering

from my asshole –
    Nude Woman with Necklace,
        you said,

but I never expected
    this ravaging,
        to become not so much

a living landscape
    as a slut-landscape,
        turned

into a jagged mountain range,
    my naked limbs
        a chaos of blood-red sunset

and sea-green forest –
    hey, Pablo, this is me, remember,
        your young spouse, Jacqueline,

facing the gauds of your raging palette –
    Rage, rage, against...
        You say I am

terrible and splendid
    as the Witch-Queen of Sheba,
        but why put such a sad look in my eye,

such sorrow in the crook
    of my up-bent right knee,
        why give me black rat's-tail hair,

black navel, nipples and asshole?
    But you, you bad old man of the forest,
        raging, raging against the dying of the light

just say – *it's all there,*
    I try to do a nude as it is...
        Thanks a lot, Pablo,

for seeing me as a nature goddess
    lounging flatulently
        on cushions of red and gold –

I lie on a painted divan,
    you hover over me,
        Zeus in a cloud,

Zeus in a shower of gold,
    my ancient and annihilating lover,
        I'll never take up this bed

and walk again,
    caught in the pincer grip
        of your angry love's yes and no,

you *raging against the dying of the light*
Yet thanks to you
I'm perfectly composed,

my perspectives
shocked into serenity,
any casual spectator in a gallery

looking into my jetblack eye
will see you, Pablo,
enraged Immortal

Behind my back,
you conjure a vast sea
riven with stark-white light

welling up and high-tiding it,
then ebbing
to richest dark blue –

You strip me bare,
subject me to your lust for life
till I'm just bones and blood

of landscape,
merely *a raw sexualised*
arrangement of orifices –
breasts,
and cumbersome limbs –

You reveal me to the core,
leave me nothing to conceal,
utterly *nue,*

but there are limits to your power,
old explorer,
despite your rage

I slip from your controlling hand
      into my own being –
            Beware – should I care to, I'll rise

from your canvas,
      crush you beneath my massive careless heel,
            like Time herself,

prisoning you
      forever
            in the world's endless gallery.

Returning a Reindeer

Here is the reindeer I stole from you months ago –
such a reindeer,
this *jieva* in her third winter, pure white,
tame, even her shadow, beautiful.

She was standing lost in thought
by the *foss*, and I just had to steal her.

I'm leaving her here outside your *kåta*...
may Mary of Lapland forgive me,
may she bless you and this lovely reindeer
and all your *raidu*,
even the barren ones, even the *heagi*
good only for hauling the sleigh.

jieva: female
foss: waterfall
kåta: home
raidu: reindeer herd
heagi: gelded reindeer

Liking

I like the silence
when I'm alone at last,
hearing
my own thoughts
however small and insignificant

I like the dawn
waking me early
for no good reason
but gladness to see me again

I like the tree
who stands beside his shadow
as the sky goes rapidly from east to west
and back again

I like autumn,
getting a life again, so I see

I like to waste my time in prayer
no matter how many times you ask me –
why do you waste your time in prayer?

Threat Register

I'm compiling my own threat register,
getting in touch with my inner terrorist,
reasoning with my suicide-bomber shadow

I'm monitoring the climate change
of my every mood, working out the quantifiable risks
of a tsunami of rage when faced with – for instance –

a household item packaged so fiercely, so resistant
to fingers, scissors, curses, knives, secateurs,
it might as well be encased in see-through steel,

    and thus,

I hope to avoid a humanitarian disaster in my own kitchen.
(Not sure yet if I should wear a uniform
when making my hourly emotional security checks) –

    box of tissues in every room – check,
    adequate supplies of alcohol – check,
    more than adequate supplies of Hotel Chocolat – check,

    list of essential numbers by the phone –
    Samaritans – check,
    Old Dope Peddler – check,

    Health Centre – check,
    Dalai Lama – check,
    Emergency Friend One – check,

    Emergency Friend Two – check,
    Emergency Friend Three – check...
    Yes, everything seems fine.

No doubt, as Government points out,
the more threats we face, the safer, paradoxically,
you and I will be. Feel safe yet?

Better To Be Water

Better to be water
  endlessly on the move
    from source to tide,

from cloud to earth
  and back again,
    or to be made of air

that also escapes,
  however fiercely held –
    better to be thoughtless fire,

or earth in its constant sleep,
  but I'm flesh and blood,
    unable to believe

the world is just as beautiful now
  as it was
    that zero-blue morning

on the clifftop at Maenporth
  when we saw
    a crystal mirage

of columned temples and palaces
  standing on the water
    through which a fishing boat glided,

oblivious of the wonder –
  Not believing the evidence of our eyes,
    we asked a passing hiker,

can you see that?
  His astonishment confirmed ours –
    there it was – skimming the waves,

a Byzantium of ice
     built from the collaboration
          of light and frozen vapour,

as if a glitter-architect was working
     with the most elusive
          and rare fabrics she could find –

               and offering it to us...

The Harper

I'm just one among millions now
in the street's city, by the sea's ocean,
by dawn's dusk and the long white nights of summer.

To stop myself thinking about all the days and nights
we'll never share,
I keep myself busy as a maternity hospital
nine months after a catastrophic city-wide power failure.

We were two among millions, oblivious of crowds,
content with our pauper-treasure,
our long-running nuptials.

But the random harper, who has but one torn tune,
has played you his tune –
now I'm just one among millions,
will never magnify the Lord again in this lifetime.

Lost for Words

I'm speechless in Iraqi, whose words drink light,
in Breton, that leaf-rustle tongue,
and in Latin, with only its darkness to see by...

I'm lost for words in Russian
hardly raising its voice above a whisper,
and silent under the long-arm charm of Yiddish bright across old
      Europe.

I spend all day putting silences in the wrong order
in one language after another –
until a brave man of letters

bears me on his broad back
to our marriage bed,
where he gives me more than my fair share of song.

Heyday

For You

These are for you, my forester,
my tired one, my unbeliever,
my believer –

Yesterday's fountain,
the last appearance of the sun,
all the world can spare of Jerusalem,
the fruit of every tree.

These are also for you,
my love, my human shield –
this something moon, this whatever sky,
these tall dew-tipped reeds from the banks of the Nile.

Husband, take my greatest treasure –
this rogue tiger, Grief...
See, he has eaten all of me bar my hands.

Handmaid

I separate my wheat
from your chaff,
or is it the other way round?

I conduct silence
like a guest
from room to room.

I lie on the heart's anvil
under love's terrible hammer
while mice nibble through
your bowstring
and rats gnaw your shield.

No human being

No human being
ever wastes time the way the ocean does,
giving in to its grief.

No human being
is ever in charge of his or her future
the way a river is.

No one's ever right about everything,
except the sun,
even when he's wrong.

No one's so easy to please as the moon,
nor so wide-awake as sleep
when war breaks out.

No one's travelled so far as you,
my love,
your voyage a knife, my heart its apple.

Nowhere

I know how summer behaves
when she's alone with the river –
that bee-queen,
proud as any red-hot opal,
biting the hand who feeds her.

But I've no idea
who I fell in love with last night
nor how my bed
got so mussed with stars,

nor why I hear and hear your footsteps
light years away from this world
where a kiss is punishable
by death, where it is raining nowhere.

Nothing

I have nothing left but tomorrow.
You have nothing left but yesterday.
So we go our separate ways.

I make my bed, lie on it,
cool my heels in sleep.

I call myself *Quiet*.
I call myself *Silence*.

I take pity on the hills,
give purpose to the trees,
become the distance
between two green towns.

I do this for you,
who watch my every move.

Cloud

I've turned my tears into a cloud,
wrapped myself in its silver lining,

turned the bitter cup of my pride
into a cask of wine rarer than hooch

brewed from the mare's-teat grape;
I've led yesterday's horse to the drinking trough,

watched him gulp down great draughts of water,
locked his stable door just in the nick of time,

and from the pig's ear of my sadness
I've woven and sewn

as many silk purses as any skilled seamstress
can manufacture in ten thousand days...

Two wives

You be the Sage Yajnavalkya
and I'll be your two wives,

the elder a threshold for the rain,
the younger plotting a world shortage of honey.

Wives full of grace,
we'll roll the single bead of our prayer

around the world for one thousand hours,
not one second less, not one minute longer.

That is what we will do.

Heyday

In our heyday,
before Grief reached out a finger
to darken all my days and works,
I was like the green tree
the goldsmiths of Paris
brought to Mary
in her great house by the Seine
on the first of May,
green tree of white blossom,
called unlucky in England,
no mother of my mother's generation
allowing it in her house –
(in the first week of May, 1955,
Mum thrusts
the fragrant branches I've carried home
into the dustbin) –
oh Peter I was like the green tree
brought blossoming into the churches of France
and laid on the holy lap of Mary Nature,
but only for you...

FB's Mirror

(for Michael Bayley)

He loves me, he treats me like dirt.
Once I was oh so perfect
but now, thanks to him, I'm bespat
with filth, vomit, paint, you name it.
I reflect his so-called deeply ordered chaos.
I'm his eye, his Ego, his agon, his O,
smirched porthole of his bar-fly soul.
He lugs me from studio to studio,
just look at the pix, I'm always there,
painting him into a corner.
Good master, will you never rubbadub me clean,
so I reflect a bright and simple world again?
Ach! As if I care. I'm your scrying tool,
your anguished sitters must all obey my rule.

Faust

If, for you, waking is like throwing open a window in a Matisse,
no hair-shirts offered,
then know you're blessed.

If, for you, afternoons are a leisurely stroll in a Russian forest
through vistas of wild roses,
then know you're living a charmed life,
friend.

If at dusk you never see the dead boy Tsarovitch go on bright tiptoe
through the topmost branches of the bonny silver birches,
call yourself lucky.

If in the evenings you receive regular visits
from The Virgin of Tender Mercies to Evil Hearts,
do not complain about your utility bills,
the credit crunch, or the indifference of your peers.

How many of them dine, as you do,
upon nightingale breasts poached in mother's milk,
prepared for you by the pierced hands of God's Son himself?

At the Hospital

Early morning, quiet and lovely September
In the hospital car park,
air slides round us, afraid to breathe

I help you walk slowly inside
to the nerve centre of fear, where hope
falls by the wayside

It takes us so long
to get you into the hospital gown
a nurse comes to investigate,

leads you away through storm-grey doors
I never want to see again
When you come out,

frail and confused,
supported on either side
by two bored orderlies,

your lips caked
with the white salts of barium,
you're shivering with a sorrow
I only now begin to understand

Somehow I got you dressed again,
your poor stiff humble feet
tangling in your corduroy jeans

On the drive home,
I hope my words were round and warm
and comforting as new loaves –

I fear they were hard and cold as stones

The barium-swallow test
came back negative –
A year later you died of other causes,

all four detailed on the black-edged certificate –
none of them the cancer you feared

Bread

I work hard for my nightly bread
even though I'm only a poet

I work hard at listening
to what my left hand whispers to my right,
and at folding swans back into ice

I work hard, praying for the stamina
of Chagall's favourite mistress,
or the happiness of a woman
married to a man without a foreskin

Hard I work,
scrubbing doorsteps and stairways
made of words

I eat my bread dry

I reach down, pluck my unknown grandfather
from the blackout air-raid streets
of 1941 London,
removing this Superintendent of a Work Gang
repairing the city's fractured water supply
from danger

I can do this,
although I am only a poet

The Train

A lake is made from the storms
it has caused all winter

A summerhouse is not to be believed in,
in January, amen...

I'm sending you messages
all the time

by spirit-parcel-post,
holi-gost kisses

from my stormy world
where Sven's men keep crashing
out of the World Cup –

You'll be happy to hear
my education proceeds as usual,

via forests and lakes,
footprints in the tide-line,

zests of light along tiny *atzacas*,
those knife-blade dead-ends,

less happy to hear
that my life is like being on a train

enroute to you
but when I arrive

where does the train ever halt
but at a platform strictly marked –

Do Not Alight Here Do Not Alight Here Do Not Alight Here?

Passaway

deep sorrow for his passaway
    sorry we lost he

after your passaway
    I give you river,
    cloud reflected in river

You give back river,
    you give back cloud

    sorry we lost he

I give you whirling dervish of house,
    half-mile of heron

You give them back,
    you are passaway

I give you memory
    of our weekdays and weekends
        and all the days in between

You give them back
    with or without sorrow
        I can't tell

    sorry we lost he

I give you hodgepodge of spiders,
    Love's dagger-proof coat,
        myself when young

I give you river and cloud,
    you return them, unused,
        don't need them

you are passaway

When the Year

When the year suddenly arrives
at June without you,
the sun boasting
of being the apple of his own eye,
I ask everyone
to explain your absence.
Silence.
The moon puts in her oar
around midnight, when you still
haven't appeared, the moon
who in her *hello-you-guys* over the sky
generates more power
than all Britain's power stations
put together. But she knows nothing
of your whereabouts, or so she says.
The rain fainting from hunger
comes along next, all ignorance and excuse.
And when I bend my ear
to the babel-song of the radio
I'm no wiser.
The year arrives at July, August,
September, with not one word from you.
By now, what a collector of months
I've become,
slowly coming to my senses,
as the year does,
having no choice
in the matter.

Burden

You gave water to the diviners,
gave Cornwall the shirt off your back.

You offered April your midnights,
handed Salome her veils.

I was not the last person to see you alive.

You insured the rain against drought,
carried the world on your shoulders.

Sometimes its weight crushed you to your knees,
sometimes you hardly noticed it at all,

one of the miraculous woes
you accepted as part of the deal,

costs you never counted –
you were the last of your kind.

White Horse, Westbury

Hang-glider over the white horse,
sun-lit rider,
gnat-small over the white tail,
flank, neck...

Green hillslope
displaying the horse,
as a green wall
holds a pure-white arras
of equine design,

a green so scarab-beetle bright
it has stopped believing
in autumn,
even though the calendar says
                October's almost been and gone

I'd give a lot to be the gutsy one
who wings it like a minor dragon
over the chalk-carven horse,

to be held aloft in blue air,
skim-buffeting the thermals,
steering unwaxen wings close to the sun

who glides his rays closer day by day
to the closing stable door of winter

Royal Society for the Promotion of Loneliness

(for Andrew Robinson and Victoria Field)

I'm often the only one
attending the AGM, chairing
an empty hall,
taking silent minutes.

There are never questions from the floor,
but mostly I keep busy,
updating the website
with its *blue-for-the-blues* screen saver.

I designed our logo – like it?
a cellist playing late at night
to a deserted Asda car park...

Our membership just hit three million,
so I'm planning our first Conference
provisionally titled –

> *Loneliness –*
> *Learned Response or Inherited Trait?*

I've found a venue
miles from anywhere
high up on a Brontëish northern moor
in mid-November.

Speakers have already been invited –

The Owl of Loneliness
(a nom de plume, I'm guessing),
The Man Voted Loneliest Man in Hong Kong,
The Woman voted Loneliest Optician in Bath –

they haven't got back to me yet,
but surely they will...

During the Conference
(every room a single room)
I've factored in a few lighter moments –

a solitaire tournament
(realistically, loneliness is not a team sport)

a quiz, the paper to be completed
in your own room, without anyone helping you –

sample question – what do you call
the loneliest dog in the world?:

a: Rilke
b: Stalin
c: Me

I'm confident that after the Conference
we'll all go away
owning our own loneliness...

Surely someone will turn up –
The RSPL is my life,
but where is everyone?
just one other lonely person will do...

Echo Village

(for Zoe)

What you loved best
was going, every Sunday afternoon,
rain or shine,
to the tiny town

where you, though only five,
were giant Athene
striding down from Olympus

through the humdrum streets
of ankle-high houses
with inch-wide curtains at their windows

and doors only a snail
could easily enter –
with what jubilation you raced

round and round
the pocket handkerchief village green,
leapt the little stream

trickling through the waterwheel
no bigger than the face of a grandfather clock –

That little world you loved,
where you played, happier to be bigger than,
has fallen from favour –

sold on, sold again, then sent for scrap,
no sign remains of where you ran,
baby houses, school, church, fire station
all tumbled away

The world is big and not a toy,
this you know –

Yet the little town in its green hollow
goes on remembering itself
whenever I pass the site –
echo-village, child's delight –

scrap of net at the window,
horned snail at the door

The Search

Pleasure hides herself from me
behind a knife-edge of rain,
in the water of one tear.

Pleasure turns her face from me,
loves everyone but me.

She dresses up for autumn,
or is naked in the arms of a stranger.

When I look for her,
she hides herself in your absence.

I bring her gifts –
a pearl of great prize,
a carefree mirror, a shoe of glass,
a book of blank pages,
a song no one but Pleasure is allowed to sing.

I cast rainbows on the ground
for her to walk on, dry-shod

but she hides
in every minute the clock sheds.

And if she hides herself
in the wilds of time
how shall I ever find her?

She hangs out with the wolves
in the badlands by the Lake of Bays,
she's up in the woods with the bears
at Sainte-Marie Among The Hurons.

She hides under the wine-taster's tongue,
in the dream's ear,
in the gay village at midnight –
vanishing uptown and downtown.

She flees from me
                    as silence flees noise,
                    ice, fire...

But when I'm past caring,
she comes to me,
tells me you're waiting for me
in that café on Humming Bird Street.

Silver Ring

Your old silver ring, Peter, was too big for the ring finger
of my right hand
so a jeweller shrank it down to make it fit.

      Love has no secrets from death,
      nor I from you.

That ring vanished for months.
I found it by chance in a box of oddments
where you'd tucked it away
the day you gave up wearing rings.

      Silver has no secrets from the moon,
      nor I from you.

You loved silver rings,
wanted no gold wedding band –
this moonstone lodged
in roughcast silver was your favourite.

      The day has no secrets from the night,
      nor I from you.

Each night I take off your ring,
draw time's fine scarf through it.

Every morning I slip it on again,
a secret never to be told.

With this ring I thee remember.

Sorrow at last

must be left to fend for herself

Her gifts were not asked-for,
nest egg of tears,

rainstick summer,
alas of words

Sorrow
must fend for herself,

like someone
who keeps on singing

long after the song
has finished

Her aviary must take wing,
her colour-blind window return to the furnace

Sorrow must fend for herself,
board the lifeboat *The Will*,
head out to sea
through steep dark-blue waves,
riding their slam-white storm crests

I saw Sorrow, beloved,
sitting in your good chair for reading,
beer-can in hand,
books piled nearby

I watched Sorrow drain the can,
close her book,
go through the door,
close it behind the both of you.

What I Want

Wrap me again
in one of your daytime skies,
clear or cloudy, dear one,
I don't care

Fold one of your nights
around me,
star-racked or starless,
I don't mind

Hide me in your second-best forest,
spring-budding or haggard with autumn,
its all the same to me

Cast one of your seven oceans
before me, beloved,
let it be Pacific or Indian,
I'm not fussy

Weave me a web,
lost one,
lodge me on a radial
that looks frail,
yet is strong as steel

Let me sway
in that bright winking maze of tears
for one hundred years

Last of all, best of all,
write me a letter, sweetheart,
be sure to put in all the syntax,
the verbs and the pronouns, that's all I ask,

a single grammatically correct love letter
in your own weatherwise hand

Student

Every day Grief sets me my lesson.
Learn this by heart, says the Professor.

My exercise books stack up,
all wrong answers and reproachful red markings.

The terms drag on and on,
holidays are few and far between.

Surely its time for me to march into the gym,
find my desk, set out my clear plastic pencil case,

bow my head as the invigilator
puts the exam paper in front of me?

Whatever dead language asks the questions,
no matter how hard the sums I must do,

surely after such coaching and cramming
I can't fail,

must graduate with honours
from this sorrowful schoolroom,

scrape a living by all I've learned so long and hard?

1923

In the winter and wintry spring of 1923,
November to March,
after sixteen weeks

first in Stanwell Isolation Hospital,
then in The Hospital for Sick Children
in Windsor,

suffering from diphtheria,
receiving very few visitors,
(her mother having little spare money

for bus fares, or time to visit
with a new baby at home,
two older girls to look after,

and at a time when visitors
were unwelcome on the wards),
my mother, not yet three years old,

is pronounced cured, and sent home.
After a few days back home,
she asks her mother –

are you really my mummy?

Eighty-four years later,
she tells me this memory
for the first time –

Such a silence falls between us
in the kitchen,
such feeling for that far-off wondering child.

For we are both mothers of a daughter,
know how a mother feels
when her own child barely remembers her,

not daring to believe she is mothered, loved...
the maternal chord struck,
a chord vibrating between us...

Were there any other children
for you to play with, on the ward?
I ask...

She thinks back...
A little boy, in the next crib
on the verandah, alongside me...
his feet stuck out through the bars,
a weight suspended from either....

Letters

Today I wrote a letter to green,
the colour I love.

My letter came back unopened,
put me in my place
like the entire refusal of autumn to speak.

I wrote letters to blue,
to red, and all his hedgerow cousins.
I wrote another letter to green.

Not a single colour answered.

Maybe they'd all moved away to a country
where rainbows are against the law,
painters lie awake all night,
and nothing is known about love.

FOR JACK SHUTTLE

five poems

Dad's Last Diary

Today I take his place at the desk,
move his old-fashioned blotter

to make room for my lap-top,
sit in his old carver chair,
to write this poem

Dad loved all poetry,
scribbled scraps of light verse,
birthday poems for his teenage sisters

posted back from Malaya in 1940,
a few valentines for my mother.
I flip through the little thesaurus

he kept for his crosswords,
then his last diary, from 2003 –

just a few entries for January,
his once-immaculate script
a large and clumsy scrawl;

Jan 3 – Colder
and some early morning sunshine;
Jan 4 – Cold and some sleet.

Then, eleven blank months,
as writing any record
became too arduous a task for the frail old man.

On these unwritten pages
I read words he's penned in time's invisible ink;

a warrior readying himself
to face anything the enemy could chuck at him.

Colours

There are many rivers
for a father to give,
forests, towers and cities

You take my dark colours
and make them bright,
bring the long-ago back to life

No car could be redder
than the sports-car in which you whizzed me
round and round town,

no green more your handiwork
than the summer's

Some colours are used by everyone,
some colours are so fragile
only children are allowed to use them,

some colours belong
in whatever world we go to
when our time here is done

Whenever I scorn my colours,
fearing them,
you give them back to me,

simply because
you are in the habit of so doing

Freed from the prison camp
for the *heavy sick*
at Nakhon Pathom in Thailand,

in August 1945
you stood at the foot
of the Phra Pathom Chedi,

huge bell-shaped Stupa,
tallest
in all the Buddhist world,

its gold-tiled dome
shining over the broken world
in the morning sun;

Jack Shuttle from Egham,
twenty-six years old,

too weak to scale the summit,
greet the Buddha of compassion,

you'd never climb hills
with ease now,
or be able to run for a bus

Yet you brought colours back,
even from Wun Lun,
Wampo South and Kanburi,

plus, you give me
a moment of suddenly noticing autumn,
a way of mourning you

with the palette of grief,
all earthly colours at my disposal

The Wand

Despite a fortnight of flu,
he was up and dressed smartly
most days in suit and tie

as all through his retirement,
(except for cardiganed afternoons
or gardening shorts in very hot weather).

Flu or pneumonia? The GP's not sure.
So Dad gets a third course of very strong antibiotics
which sparks off his tachycardia,

the rapid irregular heartbeat Dad's suffered from sporadically
since his years in the POW camps in Burma,
and now the casualty doctor (young, clever, kind),

takes his pulse,
mm, we'll send you for an ECG, blood-tests, a heart X-ray
right now...

Huh! He's had all those before,
but the doctor takes him up to Cardiac, no wheelchair,
it's a long walk,

> *by the time I got there*
> *I was panting like a dog...*

After the tests – I'll give you something
(extra-friendly voice)
to slow that heart down...

Back home, Dad soon realises the something
is just the blood-pressure stuff he's taken for years –
but a double dose.

Stop the extra ones, says his GP,
and take these beta-blockers instead, but Dad knows
they'll make him breathless and hurt his legs

like they did before
so he's put on a very low dose plus some *digoxin*
which hurts his spine so much he needs the chiropractor

to pay a home visit,
and the next heart specialist he sees tells him,
you're just suffering from wear and tear:

so yes, Dad's feeling poorly all winter,
then one day when I phone
he's feeling less-worse, and of course his famous memory

is still in great shape, if you like he'll tell you
the names of the 1927 Brentford Football team
who played at that first game

his Dad took him to,
Fox, Adamson and Stevenson,
Salt, Bain and Davies (Captain),

Foster, Lane J, Lane W, Blakemore and Payne.

My memory's slacker
but I remember the wand Dad made me,
tipped with a star of silver
when I was a little pestering fairy queen.

August 16, 1945: Yanagida surrenders and hands over command of Nakhon Pathom prisoner of war camp, Thailand, to Colonel Coates

It might not have gone so smoothly,
that handover,
Colonel Coates at once confining
the Japanese captors and Korean guards
to their own quarters,
ordering extra rations for the starving prisoners,
more rice, meat, vegetables,
an un-heard-of whole pomelo per man,
given that the Imperial Japanese Army
had orders to massacre
all P.O.W.s as soon as the enemy landed –
it might have been different,
no brand-new green US Army uniforms
and boots handed out (the boots cumbersome
after three and a half barefoot years,
or at best shuffling along in clompers),
no chance of tasting your first toothpaste
since captivity – *I cleaned my teeth*
a dozen times on the first day,
savouring the luscious flavour of Kolynos toothpaste,
I even found pleasure in just looking
at its distinctive yellow packet –
There might have been no flight
to Saigon
in the big Dakota,
with that hush filling the plane
as it over-flew the dead
in their jungle cemeteries below,
and where the railway ran, soon
to be reclaimed by bamboo wilderness –
If bombs hadn't fallen on Hiroshima and Nagasaki
(bombs of such magnitude
you and your comrades, who hadn't even seen

a Sten gun till that first chat
with an SAS man, were mystified
as to how such things could be),
or if such bombs had never been developed,
or if developed, never used,
and the war had dragged on through a long land battle,
you might not have sailed home
on the SS *Chitral*,
but like so many others,
on every continent,
never come home,
my mother moving deeper into her silence,
never to be my mother at all

Everyday Mourners

(bed, shaving brush, desk, etc)

What use am I, if you don't sleep between my sheets?

What use am I, Jack,
standing on parade for months
on the bathroom shelf, bristles stiff, dried up?

What does the future hold for me,
your old friend Desk,
now you never come to me after breakfast
to set out your uncomplicated correspondence
on my broad willing back?

What about us, trowel, fork and rake,
lined-up and ignored in the shed?

And what about me, shoved under the desk,
shut-up in my case, keyboard untouched?

Heydays and holidays come and go,
but we never escape our wardrobe prison,
six fancy waistcoats of green, gold and red brocade,
silk ties, your good suits –
a dandy's attire, you were known all over town for us

What use am I,
my one diamond bright as ever,
good as new, gold signet wedding ring
a nurse slipped from your finger,,

gave to your son,
who keeps it hidden to this day
from your widow,
who chose it so long ago

Moonspeed

Very quickly the moon shuns
the massive domes and rounded arches
of Byzantium,
the centre-fold cities of America,
Russia's cross little citadels,
by-passes backmost lakes,
all waters, cornerstones of rivers,
moon rushing
over orchards of peach and plum,
shoving clouds before her
in a cosset of shadow,
dashing over linens
draped on tenement poles,
over all your old addresses,
skimming the brightness
from each port-of-call, carrying
tomorrow's news in her breast,
along with the latent weeping of all living things,
and glittering fast, very fast over the South Pole
where the key to understanding Art Nouveau resides,
over the great Alps
in their snowy hair-shirts
and over Europe, which she salutes in passing,
coming to rest above my garden,
bringing me, whether I like it or not,
the first rain of the summer-end.

Where Are They Going?

The North Esk is heading for Musselburgh,
the Fal for the blue respite of the Carrick Roads,
without haste the Thames is making for Tilbury,
and the Nile, from her headstream
as the Luvironzo branch of the Kagera
to her splendour in Egypt, is off
to that shopaholic, the Med;
but the Humber drags himself
towards the hard-faced cold North Sea;
the Severn descends from her perfect hills
into the loving arms of the Bristol Channel,
as does the ever-loving Avon,
while the Tamar slips unnoticed
into Plymouth Sound;
leaving the oldest city in Japan,
the Basho saddens into the Sea of Haiku,
and through ice, frost and snow
the Yenisei struggles towards the Kara Coast,
and the Alma can't get
the Crimean War out of his head;
the Seine grabs the Yonne, the Marne and the Oise
by their neck-scruffs, to slum it
in the English Channel,
as that peasant rebel the Vendée
bolts for the Bay of Biscay;
the Ouse, the Yare
and the Waveney splash into the Wash
without a care in the world;
only the Danube is big enough
to make a difference to the Black Sea;
Poppa Rhine also proceeds to the North Sea,
majestic and wise,
shepherding before him the Neckar,
the Maine, the Moselle and Ruhr,
the Ijssel, the Lek and the Waal,

the Meuse and the Scheldt –
what a river!
Solitary and serene, the Po
follows his long tarnished shadow
to the Adriatic shore
and the green Mekong plays down
its cloudbursts, approaching the Yellow Sea...

Rivers, o rivers

Did I forget you, Ganges,
whose opulent delta blesses the Bay of Bengal?

Did I forget you, Tigris and Euphrates,
who marry in the broken hills
above Basra
and upon whose banks stand Mosul
and Baghdad,
rivers bearing time on their backs,
whose waters swell the blood-seas of history,
whose tides trounce the moon?

Did I forget you,
Euphrates, Tigris?

(With acknowledgements to John Ashbery's 'Into the Dusk-Charged Air')

Serious Things

Nowadays
the most serious things
come into my heart
lightly,
no dark thought
comes without its promise of light,
the way dusk
gets later all through February
until, driving maybe
towards the western shore,
you can watch the moon rise
into a sky still dazed with light.

These shadow thoughts
in my heart
are made from a sadness
that brings its own light,
spinning its round yellow moon
high into the evening sky,
so that even when night
sweeps away rocks and rock-pools,
the upper air stays vision-clear,
lifting, like my heart,
above what is lost,
up into the last of the bright
where the most serious thought
is borne up into a rich jewel of light,
a diamond on the brink
of returning to the dark matrix
from which at dawn
it will again be hewn,
polished, worn on the world's ring finger.

Sun in Winter

The sun searches the house
from top to bottom –
bright Holmes, investigating your disappearance.

He finds no clues.
Every book on the shelf has an alibi,
each bed, table, chair is blameless.

The sun carries out a fingertip search
of the frosty garden,
lifts my unsuspecting fingerprints from last night's water glass,

summons shadows to an identity parade,
appeals for witnesses to come forward;
he has many other unsolved crimes on file,

knows what good lawyers Death has to serve him,
how impossible to bring that serial killer to the gallows.

The Stove

First thing in the morning
I go out to look at the mountain,
come back in,

sweep up last night's ash
from the hearth,
sit at the table,

write to you again –
I've tried hard
to believe in your afterlife as ocean,

imagined you
travelling the globe as salt water,
but who am I kidding?

Ash is ash,
no matter where it's thrown –
I'm only flesh and blood.

Here on my own
by the black stove
whose appetite can be tempted

only by almond boughs
or the wind-chopped
branches of the little grey olive trees,

I think for the umpteenth time
how you've never seen the mountain
in its blue or sable wrap of air...

...and every morning
round about now,
Grief pads in,

electrodes at the ready,
or will it be those splinters of bamboo
under my fingernails this time?

He likes that one...

My Poet

In your poem, call me Queen of the queen bees.
Describe how I show mercy to the light,
how my honeybees marvel at their flight.
At line four portray me as a witch-bride

dancing on the bright Avon's quick bright tide.
Next, put that so-called healer, Time,
in his place, and bring song's good news
to every dumb-struck village in the land.

Here, at the volta, give Grief a free hand.
Write, my dear lost poet, and my wise –
lean your breast on the thorn of death,
separate a world's wheat from its chaff.

Tell me, only you can, why did I not die
from the bite of a snake on our wedding day?

Merchant

Who is the Shop Keeper,
and why does she never take a holiday,

dust her empty shelves
or scrub her doorstep?

Why does her shop stay open
longer than the 24-hour garage over the way?

Why does she never refuse credit,
though such generosity often offends?

Why is she never short of customers
queuing up to pay her exorbitant prices?

See her after closing time,
adding up her day's takings
by a skim of lamplight,

now and then tasting a tear,
to see if it rings true on the tongue...

Doesn't she know such salt currency
will never make her rich?

Yellow Broom

I'd rather be a black beetle
scurrying through the English Cemetery

in Rome, or a blue-throat lizard
basking in a ruined temple at Paestum

or a bat in the Grotte de Perdosa
or a ghost at her ghost-loom

weaving for all eternity
fabrics fine enough to clothe Hera,

or a *chiavi de ferro* rusted
in a door never to be unlocked

or a snail clamped to a tomb
in the long-forgotten city of Elea

than believe you're lost to me forever –
our paths must cross again somehow.

I don't care if the One who orders such things
permits you to be merely my snail-groom,

beetle sidekick or lizard husband,
or if, in some overlooked corner of the world,

Love herself recycles you as a sprig of yellow broom,
me a blade of grass lowly and glad at your wayside.

Scapegoat Song

I love the sky best on foot
when I rise from myself

like a necessary tempest,
quicker than the future,

kinder than the past,
kneeling by the mercy-seat of the light,

losing and finding
the mustard-seed of myself,

studying the deceit of pomegranates,
the doe of autumn, a leaf in its prime,

a lighthouse so white
the moon has to look the other way all night

Moon and Sea

(for John Greening)

First she arrives by rumour,
by legend, by falsehood,
     by hope

Next she arrives by rain,
     by longing

She arrives by longing,
and as if
she can't help
     herself

She arrives by cloud,
and in a mask of
     sky

She arrives
like a craze for
     mirrors,
a fashion for
     weeping

She arrives by longing,
as if she really can't help
     herself

She comes to the sea
in a rush,
     a huff,
     a tailspin,
     a snit...

Do not call her bald, do not call her
     wild,

do not say she is not a door,
of course she is a
          door –
Do not insult her by saying
          she is anyone's
          mother –

She travels without maps,
by not giving a damn,
she comes by fullpelt
          longing

She comes at her full
with a scorpion in her hand,
a knife at her breast, a price on her
          head,

unannounced,
and not always
          welcome,

arrives with her bibles that never speak of God,
          with her bitch unicorn,
                    with her heart on her
                    sleeve

She arrives without witnesses,
          without fuss,
without a care in the world,
without a backward
                    glance

She came by legend, by rumour,
she came to the sea
          by inclination,
                    by invitation,
                              by right,

she rested her Mary-sweet hammer of light on the sea

Gifts

Take my eyes, John Milton,
Take my head, Anne Boleyn

Take my arms, Venus de Milo

Take my blood,
you 'ole mosquitoes

Take my liver,
Hannibal Lecter

Take my breasts,
St Agatha

Take my tongue, Philomela
Take my shadow, sun
Take my light, moon

Take my anger, Job
My chains, Houdini

Take my hours, time
Take my silence, mother tongue

Grownup at Last

Don't confuse me with a woman,
I'm just a child's harp asking not to be touched

Don't confuse me with a mother,
sister or daughter,

I'm no longer so up-to-date,
so pliant a mirror

Like the earth,
I'm in two minds at once –
one light, one dark

Like the moon,
I'm thinking my way home

to my crust of bread and my dove,
to my wet nurse, the rain,

the beautiful superfluous muzak of grief
playing and playing,

why won't someone turn it off?

In the Tate
(for Linda)

I was in the café
at Tate Britain
when your daughter rang
to say you were dying –

I couldn't find any words

Five minutes later,
having found a quiet corner
at the far end of a big space,
I rang back, got your husband,

tried to speak more calmly,
more deeply
of you on your journey,
he said you were sleeping,

sinking,
with your son and daughter
by the bed, and him, of course,
all waiting for Rose, the Minister –

she'll say the prayers
for the parting and the journey…
then the signal broke up a bit
and I said goodbye,

thinking –
the strong cable of love
joining us
all these years
is frayed to a hairsbreadth,
Linda,
is about to snap

Alone in the empty gallery
I turned to the blank wall
and wept,

but not for long,
my dealings with tears
have rules nowadays,
as you know...

I walked from the blank
corner of weeping,
went, as planned,
into the Bacon exhibition,

into his body
(in every sense)
of work, finding painted mirrors
for this day's grief,

seeing your poor wounded head,
Linda, impressed on these canvasses,
heads harmed into darkness,

into the pain no one may forbear –
but ending for you today

In a side room
Bacon's notebooks
are set out in glass cases –
on one page he writes,

Owls with meat in a circle

As I left the exhibition
a couple of girls were signing
in front of one of Bacon's Popes –
They could neither hear nor speak.

On the Patio

I set a wineglass for you
on the steel table

a glass of air
a glass of blessings
a glass of time
a glass of timelessness

a bright glass

I set a chair for you
at the steel table,
where the sun won't blind you,
the wasps won't find you

I set a shadow for you,
I set a song –
these are the summoning things,
these are the wounds

I set a wineglass for you
out on the steel table

When rain and purple thunder
fill it to the brim,
I know you'll drink,

then bang it down
for a re-fill

You are everywhere
as rain,
ordinary as sunlight,
profound as silence,

or the moon
remembering the good old days
when she was a man

Bower

I often admire
the ruins of my bower –
    hedgebroom, dwarf birch,
    green alder,
    willows, thrift,
    yellow-horned poppy –

where I close a door
in order to study doors,
    their place
    in the miracle of light –

where I hold my breath
in order to study breath,
    its power over me –

where, like a saviour sibling,
I turn from the price on my head
to study an hourglass,
learning
    what time loves –
    the great libraries,
    Patmos, Dublin,
    Seville, Morrab, Venice –

where I travel here and there
in the twilight zone of the past,
    Danaë and Perseus
    bound in the seaborne chest,
    Azanor also castaway
    with her boy,
    the saint-to-be

I often admire the ruins
of my burnt-out bower
      where sometimes I glimpse you
      at the helm
      setting sail for Spain,
or, later, pondering
the crabbed salt-stained script
of the Captain's log
in your bower-like cabin
on the good ship Eye of the Wind...

Birthday Gift

Today, 2nd January 2008,
I'd like to give you your 76th birthday.

You'll wake early, but not too early,
feeling as well as a 76 year old can,

a twinge here, an ache there,
mustn't grumble...

I'd like you to have
plenty more birthdays,

and all the days in between,
mostly good, some bad (see,
I'm being realistic here).

I want to give you the time you never had,
by sticking nobly to your three score and ten –

all that living and learning,
writing and thinking,

walks and days out at The Lizard
or Penzance, movies...

I'll be right there at your side,
I've allowed room in my gift for me...

I'd like to give you
an amended Deathday –

let it be June 16th, 2015 –

You'll be 83, getting on,
ready to call it a day –

you always said to me,
I think I'll die aged 83,
just like my Dad.

I wish I could gift wrap this present of Time,
I know it's just what you wanted.

But no shop stocks it,
no merchant offers it.

Now, when your birthday comes round,
I turn a blind eye,

bin the calendar,
say your name, just once,

quietly,
looking over my shoulder
at the never-you who's always there,

dear shadow,
asking for nothing.

(I am indebted to D.M.Thomas for the phrase italicised above,
taken from his collection, *Dear Shadows*)

At Housel Bay, June 2002

We sat out on the hotel lawn
evening after evening

all that midsummer week,
watching the swallows,

absolute ariels
exulting overhead

in the bright sea-reflecting sky,
the long late June light

shining higher and higher
into the blue

till it could go no further,
paling to silver

where the rapid dusk-drunk birds
banked, cutting corners in the air

as the first fastidious star
rose into that radiant cloudless sky –

watching so silently
any random observer might think

you and I knew this was your last summer –
we didn't, of course,

were no wiser than the birds
in their delight, their sky-high wisdom...

So fate shows her charity,
so death hides his face in brightness...

A Singing Man

For an instant,
you're sitting on a chair made of rivers,
at a table woven from snapdragons and sunflowers,

writing songs in invisible ink
on a page the silkworm has spun you
from hand to mouth

The world's last straw drifts by

Your study folds its wings
and carries you away

But like the dove at Bareppa
I'm wrought of iron,
can't follow you,

only offer you
my olive branch,
holding it out to the place

where you, for one heartbeat, were,
        but are no more,
my singing man who keeps his shop in his throat

'The singing man keeps his shop in his throate'
– George Herbert, *Outlandish Proverbs*, No 918

119

Distance

People say you can see the stars
in the daytime
if you're down a deep stone well

I'm much deeper down
than any such well,

can see you, way up there,
looking for me,
as fearful of the heights you inhabit
as I am of my lowliness

Ah but I can't bear you being afraid

Let's not be afraid,
despite all this star-borne distance between us,
divergence of the twain

In Your Sleep

You'd talk in your sleep.
I harvested those words from the quiet of night,
from another part of the forest

In your sleep you were surrounded by women,
drifting from sagesse to sagesse,
sultan in your dream harem

Or you confronted bearded muscular rivals,
shadow-men, rival philosophers, contenders –
even asleep, you were a lover and a fighter

The phrases I garnered
were riches saved for a rainy day
I thought would never come,

but here it is –
the mizzle of dawn,
your silent ghost. Oh speak

CODA

When Happiness returns after a long absence

When Happiness returns, after a long absence,
she's a very small creature indeed,
an orderly marching ant,
scurrying beetle, or web-spinner

Let her be a spider,
learning to spin her web again,
lodging modestly behind the washer-dryer
in the back-kitchen,
earning her keep by waste disposal of flies

Let Happiness be small, busy and eight-legged
for a couple of years –
Unhappiness, step out of my house,
go back to the wilderness,
where I can't hear the rustle of your black weeds
or even the shadow of your sobs

Now, raise your game, Happiness,
slip off your spider costume,
come to me in the shape of a wren
weaving your common or garden nest

I don't ask for an outbreak of joy so major
the police are called to quell it,
just your wren-song
drawing each no-longer-endless day to a close,
chanteuse of last light,
such modest happiness I think I can bear

Penelope Shuttle has lived in Cornwall since 1970, is the widow of the poet Peter Redgrove, and has a grown-up daughter Zoe, who works in the field of renewable energy.

Her first collection of poems, *The Orchard Upstairs* (1981) was followed by six other books from Oxford University Press, *The Child-Stealer* (1983), *The Lion from Rio* (1986), *Adventures with My Horse* (1988), *Taxing the Rain* (1994), *Building a City for Jamie* (1996) and *Selected Poems 1980-1996* (1998), and then *A Leaf Out of His Book* (1999) from Oxford Poets/Carcanet, and *Redgrove's Wife* (2006) and *Sandgrain and Hourglass* (2010) from Bloodaxe Books. *Redgrove's Wife* was shortlisted for both the Forward Prize and the T.S. Eliot Prize in 2006. *Sandgrain and Hourglass* is a Poetry Book Society Recommendation. First published as a novelist, her fiction includes *All the Usual Hours of Sleeping* (1969), *Wailing Monkey Embracing a Tree* (1973) and *Rainsplitter in the Zodiac Garden* (1977).

With Peter Redgrove, she is co-author of *The Wise Wound: Menstruation and Everywoman* (1978) and *Alchemy for Women: Personal Transformation Through Dreams and the Female Cycle* (1995), as well as a collection of poems, *The Hermaphrodite Album* (1973), and two novels, *The Terrors of Dr Treviles: A Romance* (1974) and *The Glass Cottage: A Nautical Romance* (1976).

Shuttle's work is widely anthologised and can be heard on The Poetry Archive Website. Her poetry has been broadcast on BBC Radio 3 and 4, and her poem 'Outgrown' was used recently in a radio and television commercial. She has been a judge for many poetry competitions, is a Hawthornden Fellow, and a tutor for the Poetry School. She is current Chair of the Falmouth Poetry Group, one of the longest-running poetry workshops in the country.